Spelling

Pupil Book **Year 1**

Christine Moorcroft

Features of this book

- Clear explanations and worked examples for each spelling topic from the KS1 National Curriculum.

- Questions split into three sections that become progressively more challenging:

  Warm up

  Test yourself

  Challenge yourself

- 'How did you do?' checks at the end of each topic for self-evaluation.

- Regular progress tests to assess pupils' understanding and recap on their learning.

- Answers to every question in a pull-out section at the centre of the book.

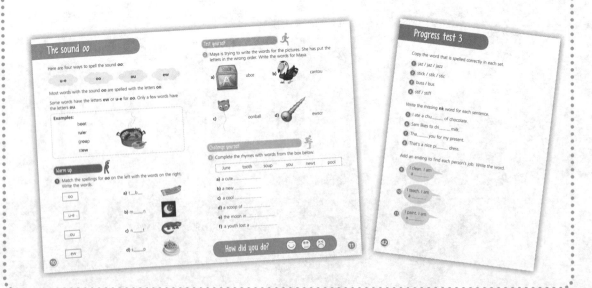

Contents

The sound *ay*

Here are three ways to spell the sound **ay**:

a-e   **ai**   **ay**

Lots of words end with the letters **a-e** or **ay**. You usually find the letters **ai** in the middle of words, not at the end.

Examples:

My n**a**m**e** is J**a**n**e**.

I'm in j**ai**l.

Tod**ay** is Sund**ay**.

Warm up

1 Copy and complete the words with **a-e**, **ai**, or **ay**. One has been done for you.

a) g_ate_

b) tr___n

c) cr__n__

d) s___l

e) h___

f) pl___

2 Copy the rhyming sentences and complete the words in each rhyme.

One has been done for you.

a) I am going to play with some cl*ay*.

b) He went to jail for stealing the m_____l.

c) The dog gave a wail when I trod on its t_____l.

d) Stay in the bay, don't swim aw_____.

Challenge yourself

3 Copy the words in the columns and say each one aloud. Match each word from Column A with a word that rhymes from Column B.

Column A	Column B
train	nail
pale	tray
away	plane

How did you do?

The sound *oy*

Here are two ways to spell the sound *oy*:

oi

oy

Lots of words end with the letters **oy**. You usually find the letters **oi** in the middle of words, not at the end.

Examples:

My name is R**oy**.

Here are some c**oi**ns.

Warm up

1. Read the sentences. Write the **oy** word that matches them.

   a) This means happiness.   j_____

   b) You can play with this.   t_____

2. Complete the sentences with words that have **oi**.

   a) You can wrap food in f_____l.

   b) The drum makes a very loud n_____se.

3 Rewrite the sentences with the correct spelling of the word in **bold**.

a) The queen is from the **roial / royal** family.

b) Simon is a name for a **boi / boy**.

c) I need to go to the **toilet / toylet**.

d) Can I **join / joyn** in your game?

4 Copy the sentences and complete the words with **oi** or **oy**.

One sentence has been started for you.

a) B<u>oi</u>l some ____l.

b) Put some s____ sauce on the rice.

c) The snake can c____l around a branch.

d) A queen is r____al.

How did you do?

The sound *oh*

Hardly any words are spelled with the letters **oh**. Here are three ways to spell the sound **oh**:

o-e

oa

ow

Lots of words end with the letters **ow** or **o-e**. You usually find the letters **oa** in the middle of words, not at the end.

Examples:

b**one**

b**ow**

c**oa**t

Warm up

1 Copy and complete the words with **o-e**, **oa** or **ow**.

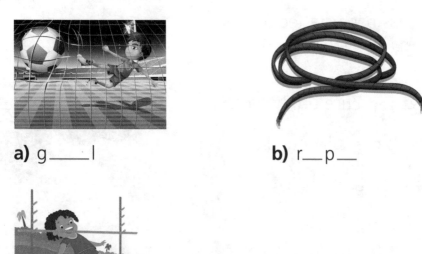

a) g ____ l

b) r __ p __

c) l ____

2 Copy the phrases and complete the rhyming words with **o-e**, **oa** or **ow**. Use the pictures to help you.

a) a m**ole** in a h_____

b) a st**one** in a c_____

c) a cr**ow** in the sn_____

d) a g**oa**t in a b_____

Challenge yourself

3 Copy and complete the words.

a)

b)

c)

I am sl_____.

Ha ha! That's a good j__k__.

This wizard is wearing a cl_____k.

How did you do?

The sound oo

Here are four ways to spell the sound **oo**:

u-e **oo** **ou** **ew**

Most words with the sound **oo** are spelled with the letters **oo**.

Some words have the letters **ew** or **u-e** for **oo**. Only a few words have the letters **ou**.

Examples:

b**oo**t

r**u**l**e**r

gr**ou**p

st**ew**

Warm up

① Match the spellings for **oo** on the left with the words on the right. Write the words.

| oo |

a) t __ b __

| u-e |

b) m _____ n

| ou |

c) n ____ t

| ew |

d) s _____ p

2 Maya is trying to write the words for the pictures. She has put the letters in the wrong order. Write the words for Maya.

a) 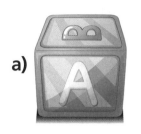 ubce

b)  cantou

c)  oonball

d)  ewscr

Challenge yourself

3 Complete the rhymes with words from the box below.

June	tooth	soup	you	newt	pool

a) a cute _____

b) a new _____

c) a cool _____

d) a scoop of _____

e) the moon in _____

f) a youth lost a _____

How did you do?

11

The sound ee

Here are four ways to spell the sound **ee**:

ee   **ea**   **ie**   **y**

Lots of words have the letters **ee** or **ea** for the sound **ee**. Only a few words have the letters **ie** for **ee**. Usually the letter **y** for **ee** is at the end of the word.

Examples:

f**ee**t   b**ea**ns   f**ie**ld   tedd**y**

Warm up

1 Copy and complete the words with **ee**, **ea**, **ie** or **y**.

a) b____

b) l___f

c) th____f

d) happ__

2 Copy the sentences and complete the rhyming words.

a) I'll **ea**t some m_____t.

b)  My b**ea**k is w_____k.

c) W**ee**ds grow from s_____ds.

d) Fizz**y** drinks make me dizz___.

e) He's a th**ie**f, not a ch_____f.

3 Write the sentences and complete the missing words. They all have the sound **ee**, but different spellings.

a) Today the weather is s_____.   b) This cup of t_____ is hot.

c) The soldier's sh_____ keeps him safe.   d) If you cut yourself, it will b_____.

How did you do?

The sound eye

Hardly any words that have the **eye** sound are spelled like the word .

Here are three ways to spell the sound **eye**:

| i-e | ie | igh |

Examples:

l**i**n**e**   p**ie**   h**igh**

Warm up

1. Match the spellings for **eye** on the left with the words on the right. Write the words.

| igh |

a) r__d__

| ie |

b) t____

| i-e |

c) th_____

2 Say the words in each list aloud. One word does not have the *eye* sound. Write the odd word out from each list.

a) tries   field   sighs

b) five   rice   police

c) bright   thief   flies

d) shield   pie   twice

Challenge yourself

3 Copy and complete the rhymes with **i-e**, **ie** or **igh**.

a) Rice is n_____.

b) a bride on a sl_____

c) I took my bike on a h_____.

d) I can't lie, I don't like your t_____.

e) a light at n_____t

How did you do?

Write the correct spelling of each word in **bold**.

1 You have paint on your **face / faice / fayce**.

2 I need to cut my **nayls / nales / nails**.

3 **Whayls / Whales / Wails** are animals that live in the sea.

Copy and complete the words that rhyme with **boy**.

4 j_____

5 s_____

6 ann_____

Copy and complete the words that have the same middle sound as **join**.

7 v_____ce

8 ch_____ce

9 n_____se

Some of these words with the **oo** sound are spelled incorrectly.
Rewrite the incorrect words, but spell them correctly.

10 group

11 pule

12 new

13 rool

Copy and complete the words with the correct spelling of the **oh** sound.

14 g——t

15 st—n—

16 bl——

Write these words correctly:

17 funnee

18 leef

Copy and complete the words with the correct spelling of the **eye** sound.

19 f——t

20 t—m—

Score ◯/ 20 **17**

The sound or

Here are four ways to spell the sound **or**:

| **or** | **ore** | **au** | **aw** |

Most words with the **or** sound have the letters **or**, **ore** or **aw**. Not many words have the letters **au**. Words that do have the letters **au**, usually have it at the beginning or in the middle, but not at the end.

Examples:

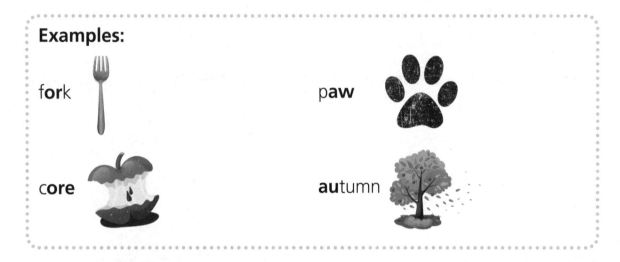

fork

paw

core

autumn

1 Complete the words with **or**, **ore**, **au** or **aw**.

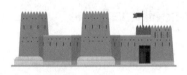

a) f____t

b) sn_____

c) s____

d) ____thor

2 Mark is trying to write the words for the pictures. He has put the letters in the wrong order. Write the words for Mark.

a) autastron

b) eessaw

c) wrda

d) strhos

Challenge yourself

3 Write the correct spelling of the word in **bold** to complete the sentences.

a) I need some **more / mau / maw / mor** paper.

b) My birthday is in **Orgust / Awgust / August / Oregust**.

c) We **saw / sor / sore / sau** seashells on the **shau / shaw / shore / shor**.

d) The **scaw / scor / score / scau** was one – nil.

How did you do?

The sound *air*

Here are three ways to spell the sound **air** that rhymes with st**air**:

are **air** **ear**

Most words with this sound have the letters **are** or **air**. Some words with this sound have the letters **ear**.

Examples:

sh**are**

p**ear**

f**air**

Warm up

1 Copy and complete the words with **are**, **air** or **ear**.

a) squ_____

b) sc_____crow

c) h_____

d) b_____

2 Help the scarecrow to sort out these words with the sound **air**.
Then write the words.

Here's a clue:
Find the letters
for **air** first.

a) rapse

b) tare

c) raich

Challenge yourself

3 Copy and complete the rhyming words with **are**, **air** or **ear**.

One has been done for you.

a) He st<u>are</u>d because he was scared.

b) There's a ch_____ on the stair.

c) I'll rep_____ the chair.

d) Hey bear, why do you w_____ blue socks?

How did you do?

Words ending with the sound v

Words that end with the **v** sound don't end with the letter **v**, they end with the letters **ve**.

> **Examples:**
>
> ha**ve**   li**ve**   gi**ve**
>
> **Note:** The **e** doesn't always change the sound of the **a** or **i**.

Warm up

1 Copy and complete the words with **ve**.

a) wea___

b) twel___

c) ser___

d) slee___

e) lo___

f) cur___

Answers

Pages 4–5
1. a) gate
   b) train
   c) crane
   d) sail
   e) hay
   f) play
2. a) clay
   b) mail
   c) tail
   d) away
3. a) train, plane
   b) pale, nail
   c) away, tray

Pages 6–7
1. a) joy
   b) toy
2. a) foil
   b) noise
3. a) royal
   b) boy
   c) toilet
   d) join
4. a) oil
   b) soy
   c) coil
   d) royal

Pages 8–9
1. a) goal
   b) rope
   c) low
2. a) hole
   b) cone
   c) snow
   d) boat
3. a) slow
   b) joke
   c) cloak

Pages 10–11
1. a) tube
   b) moon
   c) newt
   d) soup
2. a) cube
   b) toucan
   c) balloon
   d) screw
3. a) newt
   b) you
   c) pool
   d) soup

e) June
f) tooth

Pages 12–13
1. a) bee
   b) leaf
   c) thief
   d) happy
2. a) meat
   b) weak
   c) seeds
   d) dizzy
   e) chief
3. a) sunny
   b) tea
   c) shield
   d) bleed

Pages 14–15
1. a) ride
   b) tie
   c) thigh
2. a) field
   b) police
   c) thief
   d) shield
3. a) nice
   b) slide
   c) hike
   d) tie
   e) night

Pages 16–17
1. face
2. nails
3. Whales
4. joy
5. soy
6. annoy
7. voice
8. choice
9. noise
10. Correct
11. pool
12. Correct
13. rule
14. goat
15. stone
16. blow
17. funny
18. leaf
19. fight
20. time

1

Answers

Pages 18–19
1. a) fort
   b) snore
   c) saw
   d) author
2. a) astronaut
   b) seesaw
   c) draw
   d) shorts
3. a) more
   b) August
   c) saw, shore
   d) score

Pages 20–21
1. a) square
   b) scarecrow
   c) hair
   d) bear
2. a) spare
   b) tear
   c) chair
3. a) stared
   b) chair
   c) repair
   d) wear

Pages 22–23
1. a) weave
   b) twelve
   c) serve
   d) sleeve
   e) love
   f) curve
2. a) move
   b) above
   c) believe
   d) live
   e) starve
3.

D	X	Y	F	D	H	O	K
O	Q	P	M	C	X	L	S
V	F	X	M	Z	X	I	Z
E	M	A	S	S	I	V	E
P	K	H	G	L	Q	E	Z

Pages 24–25
1. a) whip
   b) wheel
   c) whale
   d) whistle
2. a) which
   b) why

c) what
d) where
e) when
3. a) What
   b) Why
   c) Where
   d) When / Why
   e) Which
4. a) whisper
   b) white
   c) whack
   d) wheat
   e) whippet

Pages 26–27
1. a) alphabet
   b) elephant
   c) trophy
   d) headphones
2. a) Joseph
   b) phonics
   c) Sophie
   d) phantom
   e) photo
3. a) fair
   b) sphere
   c) far
   d) nephew
   e) phone
   f) if

Pages 28–29
1. a) pitch
   b) match
   c) hutch
2. a) beach
   b) coach
   c) butcher
   d) hatch
   e) kitchen
   f) porch
3. a) rich
   b) Switch
   c) sketch
   d) peach

Pages 30–31
1. cork
2. seesaw
3. cores
4. August
5. dare
6. unfair
7. wear

Answers

8. cave
9. glove
10. save
11. with
12. why
13. white
14. feel
15. phone
16. photo
17. Correct
18. patch
19. much
20. Correct

Pages 32–33
1.
   a) puff, pull, puck
   b) huff, hull
   c) fell
   d) pull, puff, puck
   e) pass, pack
   f) dress
   g) jazz, jack
   h) whizz, whiff
   i) sick, sill
   j) suck
2.
   a) lock
   b) grass
   c) sock
   d) hill
   e) gruff
   f) chess
3.
   a) buzz
   b) pick
   c) hiss
   d) sniff

Pages 34–35
1.
   a) pink
   b) tank
   c) bank
   d) wink
   e) drink
   f) sink
   g) link
   h) blink
   i) ink
2.
   a) trunk
   b) planks
   c) conkers
   d) think
3.
   a) Junk
   b) blink
   c) ink
   d) blanket, bunk

Pages 36–37
1.
   a) looked
   b) cooker
   c) fixing
   d) eating
   e) farmer
   f) painted
2.
   a) cooked
   b) listed
   c) missed
   d) ended
   e) mixed
   Words that end in the sound _t_ are:
   cooked, missed and mixed.
3.
   a) dresser, dressed, dressing
   b) folder, folded, folding
   c) caller, called, calling
   d) locker, locked, locking

Pages 38–39
1.
   a) 2
   b) 2
   c) 1
   d) 1
   e) 2
   f) 2
2.
   a) 3
   b) 3
   c) 4
   d) 3
3.
   a) alligator
   b) hippopotamus
   c) elephant
   d) zebra
   e) ant

Pages 40–41
1.
   a) bed/room
   b) up/stairs
   c) thunder/storm
   d) dish/cloth
   e) black/bird
   f) jelly/fish
2.
   a) wheelchair
   b) handbag
3.
   a) windmill
   b) railway
   c) football
   d) peanut
   e) pancake

Answers

Pages 42–43

1. jazz
2. stick
3. bus
4. stiff
5. chunk
6. drink
7. Thank
8. pink
9. cleaner
10. teacher
11. painter
12. 2
13. 4
14. 2
15. 3
16. bulldog
17. lighthouse
18. toolbox
19. eggcup
20. rainbow

2 Copy and complete the sentences using the **ve** words from the box.

starve	live	believe	above	move

a) We're going to _____ house.

b) The sky is _____ us.

c) I don't _____ that story.

d) I _____ in a house.

e) If you don't eat, you will _____.

Challenge yourself

3 Find **three** hidden words that end with the sound **v**.

Write the words.

D	X	Y	F	D	H	O	K
O	Q	P	M	C	X	L	S
V	F	X	M	Z	X	I	Z
E	M	A	S	S	I	V	E
P	K	H	G	L	Q	E	Z

How did you do?

Words starting with *wh*

Some words that start with the **w** sound have the spelling **wh**.

Many question words begin with **wh**.

Examples:

what   **wh**en   **wh**ere   **wh**y   **wh**ich

Warm up

1. Add **wh** to complete the words. Write the words. Practise saying the words aloud.

a) ____ip

b) ____eel

c) ____ale

d) ____istle

2 Copy and complete the **wh** words.

a) _____ich

b) _____y

c) _____at

d) _____ere

e) _____en

3 Write a question word for each sentence.

a) _____ time is it?

b) _____ don't you eat peas?

c) _____ do you live?

d) _____ are you coming home?

e) _____ coat is yours?

4 Match the words in the box to the definitions and copy them out.

wheat	white	whisper	whack	whippet

a) speak very quietly

b) a colour

c) hit hard

d) a plant that makes flour

e) a type of dog

How did you do?   ⊗

Words with *f* or *ph*

Some words have the letters **ph** for the *f* sound.

It can be at the beginning, in the middle or at the end of a word.

Examples:

> **ph**one   dol**ph**in   gra**ph**

Watch out! Short words don't often have the letters **ph** for *f*, they have **f**.

Examples:

> **f**at   **f**un   **f**ill   **f**og

Warm up

1 Add **ph** and write the words. Read the words aloud.

a) al____abet

b) ele____ant

c) tro____y

d) head____ones

2 Copy and complete each sentence with a word or name from the box.

phonics	Joseph	phantom	Sophie	photo

a) My brother's name is _____.

b) We use _____ to help us to read and spell.

c) My sister's name is _____.

d) A _____ is a ghost.

e) I took a _____ of my mum.

Challenge yourself

3 Copy and complete the words with **ph** or **f**.

a) _____air

b) s_____ere

c) _____ar

d) ne_____ew

e) _____one

f) i_____

How did you do?

Words with *ch* or *tch*

Some words have the letters **tch** for the sound **ch**.
It is never at the beginning of a word.

We use the letters **tch** after **one** vowel letter.

> **Examples:**
>
> i**tch**   fe**tch**   ca**tch**

We use **ch** after **two** vowel letters.

> **Examples:**
>
> ea**ch**   poa**ch**   rea**ch**

We also use **ch** after a vowel letter then a consonant letter.

> **Examples:**
>
> mar**ch**   mun**ch**   por**ch**

There are some exceptions that you have to learn:

> **Examples:**
>
> m**uch**   r**ich**   s**uch**   wh**ich**

Warm up

1 Copy and complete the words with **tch**.

a) pi_____   **b)** ma_____   **c)** hu_____

2 Copy and complete the words with **ch** or **tch**.

a) bea_____

b) coa_____

c) bu_____er

d) ha_____

e) ki_____en

f) por_____

Challenge yourself

3 Copy and complete the sentences with **ch** or **tch** words.

a) If you have a lot of money you are ri_____.

b) Swi_____ on the light.

c) A ske_____ is a drawing.

d) A pea_____ is a type of fruit.

How did you do?

Write the correct spelling of each word in **bold**.

1 The bottle has a **cauk / cork / cawk** in it.

2 Jamila likes to play on the **seesaw / seesau / seesor** in the park.

3 My granny eats apple **caus / cors / cores**.

4 Write the name of the month after July.

_____gust

Write the words that rhyme with **care**.

5 d_____

6 unf_____

7 w_____

Copy and complete the words that end with the **v** sound.

8 ca_____

9 glo_____

10 sa_____

Complete the words that begin with **w** or **wh**.

(11) I'm coming ___ith you.

(12) ___y can't we play outside?

(13) Zebras are black and ___ite animals.

Copy and complete the words that begin with **ph** or **f**.

(14) ___eel

(15) ___one

(16) ___oto

Some of the words below that have the **ch** sound are spelled incorrectly. Rewrite the incorrect words, but spell them correctly.

(17) church

(18) pach

(19) mutch

(20) bench

Words ending ff, ll, ck, ss and zz

The letters **f**, **l**, **k**, **s** and **z** are never alone at the end of a short word after **one** vowel letter.

f l s z

We are doubled.

k

I have **c** to keep me company.

Examples:

off   be**ll**   pa**ss**   fi**zz**   pi**ck**

There are some exceptions that you have to learn:

Examples:

gas   bus   if   us   yes   pal

Warm up

1 Copy and complete the words using the word endings on the left.

| ff |

a) pu_____   **b)** hu_____

| ll |

c) fe_____   **d)** pu_____

| ss |

e) pa_____   **f)** dre_____

| zz |

g) ja_____   **h)** whi_____

| ck |

i) si_____   **j)** su_____

2 Copy and complete the words with **ff**, **ll**, **ss**, or **ck**.

a) lo_____

b) gra_____

c) so_____

d) hi_____

e) Billy goat gru_____

f) che_____

Challenge yourself

3 Copy and complete the sentences with words ending **ff**, **ck**, **ss** or **zz**.

a) Bees bu_____.

b) I'm going to pi_____ some flowers.

c) Some snakes hi_____.

d) My dog likes to sni_____.

How did you do?

Words with nk

The letters **n** and **k** are often together in words.

Examples:

I'm a mi**nk**.

I'm a sku**nk**.

Warm up

1 Copy and complete the words with **nk**. Read the words aloud.

a) pi____

b) ta____

c) ba____

d) wi____

e) dri____

f) si____

g) li____

h) bli____

i) i____

2 Sayed is trying to write the words for the pictures. He has put the letters in the wrong order. Write the words for Sayed.

 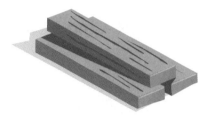

a) nktur

b) pnklas

c) ronkecs

d) hinkt

3 Copy and complete the sentences with **nk** words from the box.

blink	bunk	junk	blanket	ink

a) _____ means rubbish.

b) Your eyes _____ thousands of times each day.

c) Your pen won't write when it runs out of _____.

d) I have a _____ on my _____ bed.

How did you do?

Adding an ending

We can sometimes add the suffix **-ing** to a word to make a new word.

Examples:

   walk + **ing** = walk**ing**   play + **ing** = play**ing**

We can sometimes add the suffix **-ed** to a word to make a new word.

Examples:

   walk + **ed** = walk**ed**   play + **ed** = play**ed**

We can sometimes add the suffix **-er** to a word to make a new word.

Examples:

   walk + **er** = walk**er**   play + **er** = pla**yer**

Warm up

1 Write the new words.

a) look + ed = _____   **b)** cook + er = _____

c) fix + ing = _____   **d)** eat + ing = _____

e) farm + er = _____   **f)** paint + ed = _____

2 Add **-ed** and write the new words. Say the words aloud. In which words does **-ed** sound like *t*?

a) cook

b) list

c) miss

d) end

e) mix

3 Add **-er**, **-ed** and **-ing** to make **three** new words.

One row has been done for you.

	+ -er	+ -ed	+ -ing
dress	dresser	dressed	dressing
fold			
call			
lock			

How did you do?

Syllables

You can clap once as you say each beat of a word.

We call a beat a **syllable**.

Examples:

These words have just **one syllable**:

•   •   •

cook   mix   sing

These words have **two syllables**:

• •   • •   • •

cooker   mixer   singer

It is hard to tell what sound is in the second syllable. It sounds like **uh**.

Warm up

1 Clap the syllables of these words. Write how many syllables.
One has been done for you.

a) folded   <u>2</u>

b) waited

c) ask

d) fix

e) sorted

f) jumping

2 To read long words, you can split them into syllables. These words have been split into syllables for you. Clap the syllables, then read the words aloud. Write down the number of syllables.

a) car | a | van

b) cat | a | pult

c) cat | er | pill | ar

d) alph | a | bet

Challenge yourself

3 These words have been split into syllables but they are jumbled up. Find the syllables and write the words to match each picture.

all	e	ga	a	mus
hipp	ra	pot	tor	
el	i	phant		
zeb	o			
ant				

a)  b)

c)  d)

e)

How did you do?

Compound words

Some words are made from **two words** joined together. They are called **compound words**.

> **Example:**
>
> tea + bag = teabag

You can split compound words into two words to help you to read them:

> **Examples:**
>
> sunshine ➜ sun | shine
>
> farmyard ➜ farm | yard

Warm up

1 Copy these compound words. Draw lines to split them into two words. One has been done for you.

Read the two words aloud.

a) bed | room

b) upstairs

c) thunderstorm

d) dishcloth

e) blackbird

f) jellyfish

2 Write the word for each picture. Then join the two words to make a compound word. Write the new word.

Read the new word aloud.

a)  +  =

b) 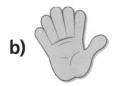 +  =

Challenge yourself

3 Choose a word from the box to add to each word to make a compound word.

Write the new words.

ball	cake	way	mill	nut

a) wind_____

b) rail_____

c) foot_____

d) pea_____

e) pan_____

How did you do?

Copy the word that is spelled correctly in each set.

1 jaz / jaz / jazz

2 stick / stik / stic

3 buss / bus

4 stif / stiff

Write the missing **nk** word for each sentence.

5 I ate a chu_____ of chocolate.

6 Sam likes to dri_____ milk.

7 Tha_____ you for my present.

8 That's a nice pi_____ dress.

Add an ending to find each person's job. Write the word.

9 I clean. I am a _____.

10 I teach. I am a _____.

11 I paint. I am a _____.

Say the words aloud. Write the number of syllables.

12 sorted

13 America

14 pupil

15 lemonade

16 – **20** Join a word from each column to make **five** new words.
Write the new words.

Column A	Column B
bull	bow
light	cup
tool	dog
egg	box
rain	house

Published by Keen Kite Books
An imprint of HarperCollins*Publishers* Ltd
The News Building
1 London Bridge Street
London SE1 9GF

ISBN 9780008184711

First published in 2016

10 9 8 7 6 5 4 3 2 1

Text and design © 2016 Keen Kite Books, an imprint of HarperCollins*Publishers* Ltd

Author: Christine Moorcroft

Series Concept and Commissioning: Michelle I'Anson
Series Editor and Development: Shelley Teasdale & Fiona Watson
Inside Concept Design: Paul Oates
Project Manager: Rebecca Adlard
Cover Design: Anthony Godber
Text Design and Layout: Q2A Media
Production: Lyndsey Rogers
Printed in the UK

A CIP record of this book is available from the British Library.

Images are ©Shutterstock.com